LAMENT FOR KOFIFI MACU

2017 © Angifi Proctor Dladla
ISBN: 978-0-9947104-1-3
ebook ISBN: 978-1-928476-27-6

Deep South
contact@deepsouth.co.za
www.deepsouth.co.za

Distributed in South Africa by
University of KwaZulu-Natal Press
www.ukznpress.co.za

Distributed worldwide by
African Books Collective
PO Box 721, Oxford, OX1 9EN, UK
www.africanbookscollective.com/publishers/deep-south

Deep South acknowledges the financial assistance of the
National Arts Council for the production of this book

Earlier versions of some of the poems have appeared in *Donga, LitNet,
Southernrainpoetry, Poetry International, New Coin, Botsotso* and *The Common.*

Grateful acknowledgment is made to Chakida Publishers for permission to
reprint "The Nurse's Eulogy" from *Wa lala, Wa sala* and to Kwela Books to
reprint "She Became the Mother Again" from *Nobody Ever Said AIDS.*

Cover design: Liz Gowans and Robert Berold
Text design and layout: Liz Gowans
Cover photograph: Andrew Tshabangu –
Bucket, Kettle, Stove on the Floor (2008)

LAMENT FOR KOFIFI MACU

ANGIFI DLADLA
(UDibi Lwase Sandlwana)

For my friends – Mpumi Beyers, Maren Bodenstein,
Bongekile Mashefane and Ramonne Mogale,
who read some of the poems or saw some
of the performances and gave me insights.

For our children and their children's children.

For you who are meeting me for the first time –
our meeting is not an accident.

Contents

I

Reptiles	11
Son from Dukathole	13
Sacrifice	15
A Short Man	19
Phrrr	20
A Great Dance	21
Khensani	25
I Failed My Children	26
Someone	28
Little Thing	30
Last Night	32
When I'm Gone	33

II

S'busiso	37
The Chicken Vendor	38
Girl from X'pilongo	39
Dog at a Shebeen	42
Letter to My Science Teacher	43
Belated	45
O Yesterday	46
Prayer in a Church Toilet	50
Prayer of the New Black Man	51
Prayer of the Wounded	52
Who Shall Bury Us?	54
She Became the Mother Again	55
When the Priest Preaches	56
Lament for Kofifi Macu	57
The Nurse's Eulogy	60
Seven Soldiers Laughed on Christmas Day	62
Song of Eza Kwakho	64

III

The Birth of Phola Park   67
Sailing to Leper Island   69
These People   72
Here   76
Something the Dead Know   77
Poet's Report to Fifa   80
A People's Constituency   82
Marikana Chorus   83
Happy Birthday   88
Bayede   90
Visitation   92

Notes on the poems   99

I

REPTILES

Our grannies told us every day
not to build houses with shiny roofs,
when we grow up, when we grow up:
'A snake, more powerful than man,
will mistake them as its lake.'
But politicians, wiser than grannies,
made oThaka township a target.

Soon sorcerers performed synchronized flying.
Crow-black clouds thickened their twist,
and bowed. Something up there, something –
Inkanyamba dragon, twisted into a rage.

Roof exploded into tangles. Like frozen
gapes of the massacred, walls gaped.

•••

Our mothers told us every day
not to use the lake as a plaything:
'A snake, more powerful than man,
is the guardian of those waters.'

One day a willowy woman emerged
from those waters, warned race-boats
skimming around: 'Stop the noise,
for my children. Play over there!'

Months later boys had forgotten – this
because they were boys, after all.
High up, a huge, corpse-like lizard leapt,
spewed viscid webs and whipped, and wrung

the boats into red specks. We stopped
our ears as we outran our shadows.

● ● ●

Our fathers told us every day
not to work in the mines of eGoli,
when we grow up, when we grow up:
'A snake, more powerful than man,
is the guardian of underworld wealth.'

Yet we worked, deep down on the inner-world
border, because we were driven, after all.

As we followed chalk marks, a white rat
with babies, circled our Baasboy, and
squeaked: 'Not that rock, not that rock!'
We downed tools; but Baasie van Tonder
never reported all this to Makulubaas.

Where we left, a night shift drilled.
One, two, three holes. A rockslide,
a breathing hole – black like the abysmal maw
of a mamba, slurped down torches,
watches, walkie-talkies.

End of mining, beginning of telling.
Pelile skati ga lo mgodi, manje
skati ga lo nyuwan mlando.

SON FROM DUKATHOLE

From Katlehong I come
by train not by taxi –
a taxi to Dukathole stops
anytime, anywhere, anyhow.
A train to Dukathole ...

I'm an alien. The residents here
are made of dust, smoke, noise.

Dukathole has an ear
of sound. Ghetto-blasters
compete with one another
blaring smoky hits,
blaring away poverty.

All is kwaito music.
No kwasa-kwasa dance music,
no mbaqanga, no reggae,
and no jazz here.

I'm an alien. Children here have
a group soul and compound eyes.

They see all
at once: The alien,
dusty games,
smoky dances,
passers-by, and
gangsters' cars.

Where is the house ...?
Who can dirt-read it?

I'm an alien,
I can't ask anyone.

'Eita Blazah!' Their greetings
followed by whistles.
I don't look back.

'For land reclamation, Blazah?'
Dusty footsteps; white noises.

SACRIFICE

1

To this day
the smell of liver
takes me back,
back to that Easter night ...

He was alone that Sunday,
my stepfather, alone with spiders
of his heart – cooking, webbing ...

2

In my childhood
when he visited my grandma
my shoulders caved in,
hairs bristled,
heart thumped,
I sweated and slunk off to the door.
In the absence of grandma
when mom tried to cajole
me into calling him "Pa",
my tongue knotted.
I cried   in the toilet.

3

I was alone with him
that night. I thought of sneaking
out to Mamelodi.
No transport.

Perfunctory inquiries ...

In the living room I took
my Olivetti and typed
meaninglessly.

I could hear him humming:
'Jesus Loves Me …'

The tune wafted with the aroma
of liver, tomatoes, onions.

I was hungry.
Minutes later he brought in
the steaming dish, and said
the grace.

4

I heard him chomp, cough, hum
in the kitchen. His cough did not
chime with flu.

Still humming, he shuffled
to his bedroom.

As I took the spoon
a voice came from nowhere:
'Do not eat this food!'

The spoon fell, and skittered
under … under the table.

Silence.

Dazed, I looked around.
Again the voice:

'Do not eat this food!'

And obey I did.

I picked up the spoon
and played at eating.

Though coughing, the man
heard clearly the hard labour
of the spoon and the tongue.
I scooped the porridge
and dumped it to the stew.
I spooned the juicy stew
and shovelled it to the porridge.
Waiting for some seconds,
I resumed my deceit
till scraping time.

Then I took it to the dogs;
but I was hungry,
dizzily hungry.

Early in the morning
I went back to Katlehong
to pack my bags for boarding school.

5

Winter holidays;
stepfather land. My eyes
landed on a desert
where the dogs slept.

'Something devilish
messed up their stomachs,'

lamented my mother,
'We tried this, we tried that
on coming back from Moria.'

I could picture Ra-Tshidi and Londi
writhing, rolling, slithering in blood
and on oozing lumps – sacrificing
their lives to show me the evil of man.

6

I left. Left home
with a living wound.
Left behind a blood
clot.

A SHORT MAN

After that inspired performance
at Wits, I was alone with the midnight
of Katlehong.

Suddenly, weapons sprang up
as if remote-controlled.

I said a two-word prayer.
They recoiled, those brutes, tripping over
one another out of sight.

I turned around.
A short man, wielding a stick,
walked me home.

I never saw him again.

PHRRR

You flew away, never bothered;
I dove and scissored through the arts,
never bothered, once we were one.

I burnt photos, letters, poems.
But your image remained,
as if you never grew.

I don't know where you are,
lost flash of insight, nightmare
of poets.

No distance, no circumstance will replace
you. We meet, oh we meet in the now
through thoughts and dreams.

Love is a crocodile, dear one,
fasting, fasting.

A GREAT DANCE

It was during the reign of Kgosi Mangope
when I first met Mmaphefo Kgetsane
in a dream we inhabited each other
at the village of Kgabalatsane.

Her breasts – two unearthly fruits –
bold as if to burst within
my hands and mouth.

Twang of panties I played
downwards to her toes –
Something of a … serenade.

With my whole hand
I measured the misunderstood.
My palm heaved – as pulse of the heart.

Our hands and tongues – keys
to hills, curves, valleys, forests,
fountains and plains unlocked
in the inner sanctum for our ambrosia.

She was a python, coiling around me.
Then we were like cows,
licking each other until we glowed
in wetness. Even the eye

of my hardened penis!
She felt and I felt watery surrender.
Greedily, she grabbed and sucked
and planted me within.

It was an elegant start
with brilliant moments —
stars reading each other
in a game of all time.

We danced a great dance. Her legs
and knees in the rhythm of ecstasy
whispered heaven to my ears.
Such was the festival of voluptuous souls!

Navel to navel we bonded,
in memory of our mothers.
We unleashed sacred delicacies
immortalizing the Earth's first couple.

I don't remember the hours spent in the firm grip
and squeeze of the python as we both moaned
and groaned and screamed and promised each other
this and that and the whole universe.

I don't remember the hours spent
before we went, dizzily, for a shower, clinging
to each other like Siamese twins and came back with gifts.
I, with a bonus of a piggyback.

It was during the reign of Kgosi Mangope
when I first met Mmaphefo Kgetsane
in a dream we blessed each other
at the village of Kgabalatsane.

She rolled me on the floor
to face heaven. There
legs apart, over me.

Her frog-jump stance
evolved into a slow dive …
ushering me into her world!

At times she would pull away,
leaving me in space
to dab or browse …

We danced a great dance;
a gentle, revolving dance
of the spheres, a graceful
choreography of all time.

We danced a great dance
of no movement at all. Only her
breathing was the way
dancing my being into hers.

Deeper and deeper I dived,
higher and higher, eyes closed, she flew with me
visiting worlds I never imagined existed.

We danced a great dance. Our buttocks,
exquisite symmetry, resonated
the sublime poetry of the pelvis.

When I was sure – Oh,
my God, out
she …!

In naked fury, we reconnected.
I empathized with her …
but I thought I was dying
in the rapture of such savagery.

Was it a seaquake?
Was it a volcano?
Was it galactic thunder
that implosion where
I lost sense of time
and lost myself?

KHENSANI

Your parents tracked us down
and whipped the desire out of us.
I wonder how you felt
the following day, scribbling
the letter jilting me.

Your parents moved you away
to a school at far-off relatives.
I wonder how you felt
far away from home,
from me.

I never heard of you again until
I got to boarding school.
I learnt that a village businessman,
thrice our age, had given you twins.
I wonder how your people felt.

In June this year, after four decades,
I thought of you the whole week.
On Friday in a dream you came –
The leggy Khensani in school uniform,
handing me an invitation for Saturday.

Five months later someone told me
that was the day they buried you.

I FAILED MY CHILDREN

They are pressing now, all five of them.
They have formed a union, against me.
The girl is the leader, the last-born.

'No manga-manga business, Dad,
no pussyfooting, we now are serious.
This December, you show the way.

'We drive you where you were born,
to the house where you grew up.
We want to capture the aura.
Then we'll be complete.

'You show us the way where
your navel cord was buried.
You show us the way where bones
of your people are rooted, our ancestors.

'Please Dad, we are no longer kids, stop playing
a politician, we know you're not
a man of Third World promises.
We want to sing with oomph our clan's praises.'

This time tears tickled down …
These kids don't understand, don't know
the wounds we had to bury
to have a smile and get on with life.

That place with its graves
no longer exists. It's now a potato farm,
so I was told. We had never returned.
We never dream to this day.

Who could return after bulldozers,
storm troopers, rottweilers bundled us
in trucks with our cats, dogs
and broken furniture to far-off locations?

These kids do not see
that part of me is dead.
Who can tell or sing about
a place that is no longer there?

How would I tell them?
Through ancient photos?
We destroyed them.
Through our books?
We could not write about that.
Through my aunts or uncles?
They are dead.

These kids are impossible. They know our house
where I later grew up. They know my parents, and
they were at the funeral of their grandmother.

My wife, my dear, why did you do this?
Why did you choose to die first?

SOMEONE

There is Someone,
or a presence,
I am not sure;
but I feel it
driving me – a voiceless
passenger, in cycles.

Sure of my way,
I sometimes feel
like changing track
as if there's a radar within.
I dodge wounds, tears;
I bump into friends, stairs.

Deaf to the feeling,
I dive, dive deep into a den
of fangs and claws. Calm, I escape.
Then I tremble, I sweat.
Neither my wits nor my muscles
could shame such death.

As youths we always plunged
into a canyon – home of a two-headed
monster. We defied parents and passers-by;
but today I would never, ever try
even if promised to win a lottery!

The other season I was deep
in the heart of flames
where fury is pumped.
I burned man, I burst into flames
with no help even from the God
of Shadrach, Meshach and Abednego.

Today, those flames are within,
lighting the path for people
between life-and-death,
between snipers and strikes.
So, Someone, or, this presence,
is older, wiser than reason.

It has paws
obeying cat's laws –
soft as placebo,
light as pumice,
hard as claws
to tend, condition,
goad, and launch!

LITTLE THING

Little thing, little thing
where are you from
as you pop up on my lawn,
in front of poorest me?
I thought you were a butterfly.

Then phrrr … a miracle in the tree.
So tiny you are, the size of my thumb.
O, turquoise-green bird,
I've never seen you in pictures;
nor read a footnote on you.

Thumb-bird, thumb-bird, I hear
twitters, chatters, chirrups, coos
and flaps; but you simply will yourself
from branch to branch in whispers
of whistles that overwhelm me.

Thumb-bird, thumb-bird, I sense you
willing yourself from tree to tree.
Slow down, breathe not your song.
Ah! there you are above the rose.
Did you teleport yourself?

No, no, no, that is not how
to hover, not how to flutter.
Are you a magical bird, thumb-bird?
Such stillness above the flower?
Such feat is from another world.

Thumb-bird, thumb-bird,
are you a visiting-entity
of smallness and modesty
from the Son of God?

Verily, verily I cast my poetic
farthing into the treasury.

LAST NIGHT

Last night I wasted no time;
I hovered over the mortals.
One was in soft snores, the other
a Pharaoh in stiffness.

For weeks I had been preparing
for this up-flight! Up, up
through the ceiling
I defied gravity.

Somewhere in another realm,
two creatures stood in my way –
demons, unlike anything in our orbit.

Each carried plate-like lips: huge round things
stretched out, and stuck to each other. Cumbersome
on those bodies, the size of Tasmanian devils.

Like frilled lizards the creatures stormed at me.
Lips burst open, displaying a furnace
with flaming teeth.

'Devils, devils!' I charged,
'All my life, alone, I have been venturing out …'
Off they backed like hyenas.

I resumed my voyage.
Screeches, menace: those creatures again.
'I am Udibi, the courier-poet of God!' I shouted.

Their tails melted away between the legs.
Their lips, like hairs in the grave, lingered.
Peacefully, I continued my voyage …

WHEN I'M GONE

When I'm gone
do not plant this body,
it will never grow
and never be coal.
When I'm gone
do not burn this body,
it has already warmed
and lit up the world.

When I'm gone
lay it naked
on a rock by the river.
That's where it belongs
in the natural world
among forests, rivers and minerals,
among voices I hear when I'm alone;
still as a statue.

When I'm gone
let shamans and sangomas
burn incense
for the spirits of the wilderness.
Let poets sing with echo-drums,
while grey-heads carrying grand-infants
ululate and dance, the sacred dance
of the Great Beyond.

When I'm gone
officious mourners;
politicians and their praise-poets,
newsmen and their cameramen,
well-positioned writers
who cramp other writers,

let them all remain armed far
at the gate.

Through binoculars, tourists will witness the sun,
frost, thunderbolts work together with life
transmuting my body into solid poetry.
Tourists will witness predators
gobble my brain to extend theirs,
gobble my tongue to refine theirs,
gobble my heart to purify theirs, and
a tree in resins depositing my seeds.

When I'm gone, my rays will still be
on their way … to reach you.
We'll smile and nod together
while bone sages debate my soul-prints,
while monkeys play flutes with my tibias,
while cubs rehearse hunting with my skull,
while tiny creatures take refuge in my bones,
celebrate sex and hatch in my bones.

II

S'BUSISO

Hefty like a buffalo calf
and older than himself,
this bright-eyed,
broad-shouldered toddler
does not welcome help.
He knows everything;
though he cannot read.

You buy him a toy,
he unpacks it
and makes it work
the way he wants.
If it fails to obey
he fights the damn thing, fights
himself, cries and vomits abundantly!

THE CHICKEN VENDOR

The bald vendor at the marketplace
with a feathery stench of stuffiness,
will coax you to his brazier and tout you
to pick out two from the cage of wire:

'One for the grill, one for your fam'ly.'

You choose, the chicken is simply tugged
by the naked neck. That cluck
you hear, a midwife once said
'is the reversal of a birth-cry.'

With a slick tying, he blends
legs together and pats you
on the shoulder, 'No chicken in town
is so divinely tasteful as mine.

'It doesn't take time
preparing it to the pot.
It doesn't take long
softening it to the bone.

'This red skin, beaded like a tongue
of a tiger, activates glands of your tongue.
Softness of bones, prize dainty – rich
in calcium and vitamin B.

'These scaly legs you're holding,
are your snack at work.
Package now yours in toto.
Come again, my friend,

I'll braai for you, gratis, mahala!'

GIRL FROM X'PILONGO

Since we left Germiston,
she'd been contesting with the stereo
to the tune of 'Xibelana':
'Buy one, you get two
fresh fruits of the tropics.
Try one and get cured
dry mouths and faces.
More buys you all make
deprive a doctor.'

That she was shrewd, was obvious.
That we all chewed, was inevitable.
Since we started, our faces had been
awash with mangoes, papaws.

'When spring revisits up north,
for rain we sing and dance,
dance and sing for blessings
we plant and sow, sow and plant.'

The taxi driver switched off his player.
It was obvious she'd won his heart.
Smiling and chewing, he sang
to the tune of 'Cothoza-mfana'.

'At sunrise down in Msinga village,
we entertain seedlings and crops
with the anthem, anthem of old
on a moving, moving rock.
At Sgodini down in Msinga
we sing bye-bye, bye-bye
to the bleeding, bleeding sun,
with the dancing, river rock.'

As the taxi passed through Bedfordview,
the girl, eyes twinkling, pointed at a house
and ad-libbed a Muchongolo tune:

'In the mind of my heart
this house has a foundation.
In the womb of my mind
this large house sprouts
as from now. Like fruit trees
in dry spring I'll not wait
for any drop, any drop of rain.
In perfumed colours I'll perform
Muchongolo with Bedford-
fordview birds.'

We all shrieked and guffawed.
The driver, replied with a Maskandi piece.
The girl followed with a rap.

'Ears of Klevahs,
shut in concrete jungle,
cannot hear the peep
chorus, crack dance
of beaks announcing a leap
to the open, open sky.

'Ears of Klevahs,
sunk in concrete, concrete shame
cannot free heart of brain,
brain of heart to inspired, inspired dreaming,
to revealed, revealed feeling.'

That was years ago.
And now ... ah, there, the kids!
Black kids and minibuses in the yard,
the yard of the house, the mansion house
in the song, the song-girl
from X'pilongo.

DOG AT A SHEBEEN

Not a tongue out, not an ear up;
just lying, head on splayed paws.
Not a lick, not a wag, not a swap;
just there, though not in chains.

He is used to the ways of drunkards;
used to extras – hobos slinking bonewards.
Only when a spray of their urine gains
him, does he whimper and inch backwards.

There is something of a sting
about that cry, that inching;
something haunting, wringing
about his rheumy eyes.

God, if a shebeen is a dog's hospice,
man has evolved, intoxicatingly backward.

LETTER TO MY SCIENCE TEACHER

Dear Ma'am, you tried hard, but deaf
were you to the eloquence of silence.
Since my father failed to be healed –
thus was expelled from the hospital
his health now falls on me.
My back and shoulders, *eshuu* – are painful;
my little legs and feet, *eehh* – are heavy.
I suspect I'll have elephantiasis.

My father does not want to hear about hospice,
'Leave me … alone, Muofhe, just … go to … school.
I insulted … ubuntu, I – auctioned – my wife … off there.'
Anything said about drugs or hospice,
he'll simply reject it point blank.
'Leave me … alone, Muofhe, just … go to … school.'
His bull-size eyes, frozen as if in invisible ice
frighten me like a spook-mathambo.

Writing a letter to one's Science teacher
is daunting. Yes, it is true, Ma'am
as headmaster Sdorofiya calls me,
a visitor from outer space landing at her own time.
'Teachers with canes, hoses, fan belts
swish off African time!' I always offer
palms, back, shoulders, without a word –
A feast for vhoSir, vhoMa'am!

When someone is dying, writing, *eish!* just dries up.
Main worry is the headache. My father bellows
and calls it, 'Thunderbolts … splitting
my– my … 43-year old … head.'
This drives the house crazy.
I mean my younger sister and myself,

for my brother inherited his truck
at T & T Transport.

I've been writing this letter for weeks.
Remember, we have been cut off. Debts
for defying Presidents Botha and De Klerk.
Our Metropolitan Council demands ninety nine
thousand rand, otherwise a Sheriff, and
Red Ants will, will– Oh, my God.
At times, Ma'am, I adopt your "Anti-God;
anti-Ancestral-Spirits" stance.

Through herbs and holy water I've conquered
sores and bleeding. He eats now, and enjoys
herbal soup from our neighbour, Aunt MaPodile.
He rattles about, and says in a breathless, raspy voice
as if falling deep, deep into an abyss,
'I'm … a … warrior, my … my daughter.
You'll … never … drop … out.'

Science Ma'am, masters everything;
but not this capricious Cape Town
weather. Now fair, now freezing,
now stormy, now scorching.
I'll be back Ma'am, after the ten days.

BELATED

At all funerals
the young man of KwaThema,
without a word, pushes
aside priests, pall bearers
and the bereaved
as if they are underbrush
and vines in a rainforest. Then,
in great pain, he wails:
'It's not him   in the shoe!'

At all funerals
in all weathers
for all eternity
the lone youth, earthed
to the graveyard
without a break,
will honour the appointment.

At all funerals
in all weathers
the comrade of the graveyard,
without a warrant,
searches hard his suspect. Then,
gutted and broken,
he totters to the anthill
and turns into a mongoose
sentinel of the Kgalagadi.

O YESTERDAY

I

Eish! this Kiss-Madolo in shorts;
obese and amoebic, shakes
the earth like an elephant in haste.
O blessed deformity
gorging on a McDonald's burger –
you are oblivious to me, a skeleton
slouching against a stranger's car!
The way to the mall gate is far.
I'm like a fountain groping to the ocean;
my body is a battleground.

Long is the distance to my Mercedes.
Were I that Kiss-Madolo,
three hours would be three minutes.
O come, dear chauffeur of mine,
come, drive me home;
home of sleep-gazing
at the ceiling.

II

I have money, money, money
but cannot buy Health and Yesterday.
Scientists and professors,
shamans and prophets
far and near – all wizards
have failed the test
to trace, trick, trap
and kill or just let the tribes
of viruses part from me with part
of me as lizards do with ease.

III

O Yesterday, buy me out, yesterday.
Yesterday, six months ago
I got a golden handshake.
That top position had launched
my mansion houses and led me
to direct consortiums and foundations.
That top life attracted women
of all sizes and colours to me.

O Yesterday, buy me out, yesterday.
Yesterday, when we arrived from exile,
our black masses could not believe.
It was as if we emerged from the Old Testament
the way they celebrated.
It was as if the heavens were showing up.

O Yesterday, let me buy you out of my life, yesterday.
Yesterday, exile where a great citizen
of metropolises I was – already
I knew. Two of my mistresses
died. Four followed
my first wife.

O Yesterday, let me repossess you, yesterday.
Yesterday, here as a student
full of dreams – brilliant
and mercurial, I wanted
to be a scientist, a top scientist!
But in me inevitable flames raged
as apartheid condemned us to death
while in song it romanticized life.

O Yesterday, let me repossess you, yesterday.
Yesterday, there was this guy ...
Ah, KK – Karl Karapau!
Karl of all answers,
Karl from Bush Varsity,
Karl who sang the *Communist
Manifesto* and *Das Kapital*
as if they were *Nkosi Sikelela*.

                    IV

I know, I know I'll die
a lonely death. Pain
is seeing noisy predators
plundering your estate –
You, a mummy, rattling. Pain
is knowing you'll be buried
with pomp, sponsored lies and extremes –
You, a mere podium for spin doctors.

I know, I know diseases
from our witchcraft
to floor one making love
with someone's wife.
But this, this virus
gorging me, like hungry hagfish,
has nothing divine within.
Only the Devil can unleash
such explosive witchery
of mega-slaughter, mega-suffering.

V

So ends my obituary.
This is the path I have travelled.
Yours in the making
to be where you'll be.
We are all rivers …

PRAYER IN A CHURCH TOILET

We wish wee, we waz deh Beeshop's Chillen;
deh God of Izryel, he woud do deh res'.
We wish wee, we waz Politishen Chillen;
to Elit Schools wee, we woud dhrive.
We wish wee, we waz bhorn to Eggzayls;
inheritahs to Hi Konnekhshins wee, we woud bee.
We wish wee, we waz from deh Oryen';
yoga it woud meyk us sabtli.
From infinit slum shackhs wee, we come;
named aftah dem Hevvy Politishens, wee deh shackhs
chillen: Dis iz deh time, pliz, show dem enjel feys,
oh Gabhryel of long agow!

PRAYER OF THE NEW BLACK MAN

Dear loving Lord of Hosts,
they say I'm hard, those with no calcium in their bones.
They say I'm fat, those with flies on their faces.
They say I can't even jog, didn't we vote out
white police and their racist dogs?
They say I'm forgetful, those still trapped in slums
that look like gums with rotten teeth.
They say I'm slow, don't they know how long
it took poor whites to be part of the ruling class?
They say I'm a dancing sucker, those irrelevant Marxists,
Africanists and their goat-smelling hooligans,
all with inchoate skulls who are still –
Excuse my callousness, King of Kings,
what they envy are my fatted shares.
Amen, till the Second Coming, Amen!

PRAYER OF THE WOUNDED

Almighty Father,
Healer of the double-wounded,
hold this hand – charred
in this freezing freedom.

Is it true, is it true Father, this thing,
this resurrection thing?

Merciful Father,
imagine Flames of Tyres
out of shameful graves
lunging for People's Pyres
to preserve People's Tyranny
of ritualized Self-heroization, Self-hatred.

It won't work, it won't work,
this resurrection thing!

Imagine God, Mango's disturbed yokels,
SADF with its mercenaries, the police
with black-hating rottweilers, jumping
berserk out of their graves.

'strue God it won't work, it won't,
this resurrection thing!

God, just imagine, Jan van Riebeeck again,
Sir George Grey and PW Botha,
the Total Onslaught-men, and the Man
of Integrity playing King Dingane.

No God, it won't work, it won't,
this resurrection thing!

God, just imagine, the Truth Commission preaching:
'So soul-fulfilling and healing to weep and forswear,
to forgive and forget!' Yet, the death-monger there
remains poker-faced with his truncated tales.

No, God! With such reprise,
no healing in our lifetime!

WHO SHALL BURY US?

Who'll close our eyes?
Who'll bury us?
We hoped they'd be the ones
who shall close our eyes,
who shall bury us.

All over the country, eMatrasini,
this song, replacing the national anthem,
bears an accent of disorientation
from the tongues of our senior citizens.
This spontaneous song,
is like the song of the ocean.
No wave has a copyright.
Only Minister Hodoshe declaims
his 'Adopt a corpse, embrace ubuntu!'

Who'll close our mouths?
Who'll bury us?
We hoped they'd be the ones
Who shall close our mouths,
Who shall bury us.'

All over the country, in every house,
the way they skeletonize,
makes life empty, meaningless.
The way they die,
demystifies, simplifies death.
The way we grieve, we joke
about death. Only Minister Hodoshe
is seriously chanting, 'Adopt a corpse,
embrace ubuntu!'

SHE BECAME THE MOTHER AGAIN
(WA PHENDUKA UMDLEZANE FUTHI)

She became the mother again
to her daughter of 47 –
Changing nappies;
washing her,
force-feeding her …
And, Lord, she sighed
on that sleeping mat!
She became the mother again
to that city misfit.

In they came with gods and wisdom.
Out they came touched, drained and haunted.

She became the mother again
to her grandson of 23 –
Changing nappies;
washing him,
force-feeding him …
And, Lord, she sobbed
on that sleeping mat!
She became the mother again
to that prison drop-out.

In they came with gods and wisdom.
Out they came bent, exhausted and wounded.

She loved them all;
yet they left her alone
with the same disease, and the stench
of bedsores …
This woman of 1920.

WHEN THE PRIEST PREACHES

When the priest preaches hell,
he always revives in me that holiday
our school visited the abattoir.

Little boys in short pants,
little girls in long gymslips –
all with pens and notebooks.
Headmaster in front,
teachers at the sides,
senior teachers at the back –
all drive us to the field of slaughter.

Between the stench of blood
and praises of blades, cries of goats,
cattle and hogs unsettle our heartbeats.
Through passages of posts, men goad,
shove forward dementedly live animals
to witness dying, and crimson bodies
on conveyors, drizzling …

When the priest preaches hell,
I always smell squelches of boots, and
I scramble outside … coughing, retching.

LAMENT FOR KOFIFI MACU

He gave me a kiss, at Balfour station
a bye-bye kiss. The train took him
away to June 16, away for June 16.

When we returned to Seme Secondary,
no coaches had any trace of Kofifi Macu.

'Your desk is cold Kofifi,' screamed
my telegram: 'I am a candle without
a wick, cold as a whistle, as a whistle.'
A registered envelope followed:
'Seme cries for you, Kofifi Macu.'

Through *The World* and the *Weekend World*,
Seme combed, examined images, read
between the lines, and furrowed its face
to dialects, jargon, sounds of words.

O, June 16, June 16, you separated us.

In December I cried as a baby,
as a baby on Kofifi's mother's breast.
'He'll come, my girl, he'll come back.'
Her plump palms echoed my whimpers.
'All over Soweto and Alex, bloodhounds
and informers hunted and haunted them.
Now no Boer can dare, my girl,
not in Mzee Nyerere's schools.'

The following day I left for Balfour.
What an enigma boys are.
Even Kofifi's friends had an interest
in me, and a few unhinged teachers.

O, June 16, June 16, you were apartheid.

I immersed myself in my studies.
Got position two in Form Two,
passed Junior Certificate in first class,
passed matric with distinction,
got a bursary for nursing
to match Kofifi's exile education.

I waited and waited for Kofifi, for a letter.
I waited and waited for him, for a dream.

O, June 16, June 16, you stole my dream.

Come 1990, come kiss of the decades …
Like ancient gods, exiles landed,
unexpectedly. They kissed the soil,
waved at the southern sun,
sang the anthem of the south.

'Kofifi's a guerrilla, isn't he?' assured
his mother, dreamily, 'He'll come back
underground-style!'

We pestered some individuals …
We haunted the movements …
One officer gave us hope:
'In exile they received new names.
Wait for us, mother,
wait for us, sister.
Once we settle down,
we will let you know.'

O, June 16, June 16, you shattered my life.

At the private hospital I tried to love
someone – a specialist, but oh, God,
the affair ended like a bad dream.
No one could fill Kofifi's space!

Come 1994, I won't vote, my Kofifi
will tell me whom to vote for.

●●●

On the election day, a white
envelope in the morning;
our surprise at the gate.

'Dear Mrs Macu,
I hate to confide this to you:
They purged him, with scores
of others in exile.

No one among us
knows their graves.

Shhh … those who gave the orders
have hidden this from God.
They will cut off my tongue,
my nose, my ears, my limbs.

Yours anonymously,
Shhh.'

THE NURSE'S EULOGY
(To Bethuel Tladi, De Deur, 11 January 2003)

Last hours, those hours!
Deep in him was the sun,
the setting sun a miracle
of glow. The gloomy cubicle,
the whole ward uncurled
into corollas of smiles.
Curtains pulled back,
bees, birds, butterflies outside
gave a hovering ovation.
Oh, how I wished to be Ntate Tladi!

Last hours, those hours!
Ntate Tladi was a miracle –
His toad's eyes were pearls on that face;
his voice, the snowflakes onto a thatched roof,
his smile, like the softness of a crescent moon,
evolved into a richness of a rumbling thunder.
He always had a humorous way of saying things;
but in those last hours he excelled –
telling tales and dreams of yesterday.
Oh, how I envied Ntate Tladi!

Last hours, those hours!
Ntate Tladi was a miracle –
Not in pain but in peace with himself.
There was something transparent,
something childlike, transforming the whole ward.
At 10h30 sharp, he asked for a glass of water.
To the tap I danced, a fish eagle
gracefully banking its wings
for its landing field.
Oh, how I wished to exude that peace!

If Death is what I saw, Death is peaceful.
If Death is the Death of Ntate Tladi, Death is beautiful.
If Death is Death, Death is not Death.

SEVEN SOLDIERS LAUGHED ON CHRISTMAS DAY

Seven soldiers came visiting
on Christmas Day, on Christmas Day,
overflowing with presents
on Christmas Day, on Christmas Day.

They punched, hung the man naked
to the beams of his hut. Head down
like a mutated fruit bat, he swung
on Christmas Day, on Christmas Day.

They circled him in urine,
laughed at the man, sang:
'I saw three ships come sailing by
on Christmas Day, on Christmas Day …'

With shreds of underwear,
two gagged the woman;
two pinned her arms to the floor,
two stretched her …

They laughed at the woman.

The toothless unzipped his trousers
and displayed a pale erection
to the man dangling on Christmas Day,
on Christmas Day.

They cackled at the man.

'Hands off my wife, devils,
hands off my–!' He spat
blood at the parading limb
on Christmas Day, on Christmas Day.

They guffawed at the husband.

'Devils,' cried the husband,
'you'll pay for this, you …!'

They chortled at the woman.

When all seven had had enough,
they marched around the man.
Left hands saluting, right fingers rubbing
the friendly weapons, while pissing:

'What a friend we have in Jesus …'

Pitching a coin as stipend in measured
bows and salutes and waves,
each intoned rounds of 'Ta-ta,'
rounds of 'Izandla ziya gezana.'

SONG OF EZA KWAKHO

You are back, as in a dream,
with that fire of yours,
now glowing with time.

Give me the file of your life,
your journey, your family.
I'll open mine.

Oh, rise higher, lover
of long ago, don't rubbish
the vows, the rites of our shrines.

This chance moment must not
empty us, dirty us, and dishonour
our marriages.

Don't go that route, lover
of long ago! Next to you, oh!
I'm vulnerable, vulnerable.

III

THE BIRTH OF PHOLA PARK

Today is not an ordinary contest. This day of truth, of nothing else but naked truth. Today is today at Dunusa Park.

The soldiers have already cordoned off the squatter camp – razor wire, horses, armoured vehicles, bulletproof vests, rifles, bayonets and, silence, deadly stillness waiting for one thing.

Without a song or dance, they emerge – the women of Dunusa Park. Without placards or flags, they advance – the women of Dunusa Park, naked from crown to sole.

Click, click, click. This is the mother of all contests! The grannies, the toddlers, the youngsters, the sisters, the mothers, the aunts, the mothers-in-law, the daughters-in-law. The short ones, the tall ones, the svelte, the nubile, the bulky, the lean, the obese, the creaky.

Some sporting huge bottoms, others carrying huge breasts; some carrying invisible bodies, others carrying visible ones; some on crutches; others on wheelchairs; some sickly, others mentally challenged.

Like waves they advance. Hundreds to the north, hundreds to the south, hundreds to the east, hundreds to the west, hundreds and hundreds of raw waves in the landscape. All with the majesty and equanimity of she-elephants.

Click, click, click.

At the military academy, it's clear soldiers do not have this in the curriculum. To win, the apartheid power needs alien intervention.

'Gaan trek julle klere aan! Go put on your clothes!' roars a loudspeaker.

Click, click, click.

'Wa thint' aba faaz, wa thint' im bokodoo – You provoke the women, you provoke a millstone.'

Horses retreat, she-elephants advance. Tanks retreat, breakers advance.

'Ek gee julle twee minute,' shouted the loudspeaker –

giving them two minutes to show them the terrorists!

'Wa thint' aba faaz, wa thint' im bokodoo!'

'You're all under arrest!' thunders a helicopter voice.

'Siya phola la!' trumpeted the women.

'Wa thint' aba faaz, wa thint' im bokodoo!'

'Wa thint' aba faaz, wa thint' im bokodoo!'

The apartheid vests retreat and retreat and retreat, and melt away from the bodies… devoid of aprons.

SAILING TO LEPER ISLAND

Here I am, today passing through Leper Gateway;
free with seagulls, waiting for a free ferry. With us
are tourists that paid for Garrison Church weddings;
for shades, thought forms snapping,
for reading Jan se Gat back in time.

Today fathers are not here; they will be here.
This I pick up from the seagulls' song,
read it from the dances of the breakers:
'*Makana* and *Autshumato*
rickety like *Granma* in Havana,
are with us, with us
not as a province in Cuba.
Autshumato, Krotoa, Stuurman
are here, here with Sheik Madura
are here, here with Imam Said
are here, here with Imam Guru
not as a paper of the Party.
Makhanda, Maqoma
are here, here with Dilima
are here, here with Fadana
are here, here with Langalibalele
not as a footnote in a folktale.
John Nkosi, Jafta Masemola
are here, here with Harry Gwala
are here, here with Leo Sihlali
are here, here with Muntu Myeza
Andimba Toivo ya Toivo …
O, *Makana*, *Autshumato*
are now here, here …!'

We sit on the shivering deck and sail,
pulling behind a bridal gown of foam.

Gales slice my ears and nose.
Gales shave my head and cheeks.
No scarf, no windbreaker, no cloak,
just like the ankle-welded prisoners – lepers
who wore boas of spiky rings.

I hear their vows in the cold clanking
of leg and arm irons, feel out their hearts
in the rings and chains that bleed.
I see in the shape-shifting waves
captors' eyes in darts and jerks
as if herding hyenas and mambas;
captives' eyes as moonflowers and morning stars
as if they are not in the thick of transplanted Christianity.
Behold, lepers' eyes receding from colonial culture
as if wolfed down by the disease itself.

The heart of the wind fast-forwards
cured criminals let loose to gentle captives.
Sweet things dangle in prisoners' faces,
scientists in the mainland prepare concoctions
of slow death to those failing to be broken in, and dark,
dark secrets in vaults, signed, with initials on, oh no …!

Page by page in the ether, in the clouds above and below,
I read lost dreams and visions of early lepers unfolding
in increments like Sobukwe's Clause of claws.

I close my eyes and cry deep into my soul,
'Who will listen to revolutionary perspective,
if in our narrative ex-Islanders only wheeze
in their comas and near-death experiences?'
I look up to the sky and cry, not because I am a crybaby;
but for what is going on in me. 'Do I figure or feature
in the poetry or art-forms of this waterscape?'

Down into the ocean depths I look.
Behold, a hand sprouting from the peak
of the mountain. From its fingertips
tentacles of words sparkle upwards:
'Enslavers have stored themselves
in the bodies of your fathers.'
I cry long, long, long tears ...

We arrive on Poqo Island.
The gulls sing the dance-poem of the Island:
'*Makana* and *Autshumato*
rickety like *Granma* in Havana
are with us, with us ...'

Against the shore surges dance.
Around Table Mountain fog coils.

'Welcome to Robben Island:
We serve with pride!
Ons dien met trots!'

THESE PEOPLE

You sense something, something wormy
about these people?
How do I know?
Come on, look here –
into my eyes.
You, in my eyes?

Ah-hah! there's you in me
and me in you,
that's why you sense something,
and surely, it always turns out to be true.

Once I was invited
to the Emperor's Palace.
They looked above my head,
these people with their teenage concubines.
I greeted them – into space they stared
jangling keys – these big cats
with bulimic bimbos
in see-through dresses.

I am not a Private Jet,
nor a Ship of Dreams.
I am not a Limousine,
nor a Hummer H4.
I am not a Country Club,
nor a Rodeo Mark.
I am not a Scion of an Eton-trained
Chief, nor a Son of an Exile.

I am the one within you,
boldly transcending
in times of bloodshed,

famine, epidemics, storms,
quakes and volcanoes.

You are the one within me,
patiently empowering
in times of fear, betrayal,
heightened arrogance,
insult and calumny.

My turn came.
I performed. Yes, I performed
at that banquet.

Everybody stood up:
The emperor and empress;
kings and queens,
presidents and first ladies,
jesters and praise poets. Even
diplomats clapped hands
and jostled for a feel
of my appliquéd jacket
and my signature beret.

Tentatively, these people
stood too, sucking thumbs.

Three times the chair hugged me,
seven times the empress quoted me.
Blasé was I with hugs, kisses and handshakes.

Then … these people
remembered me, vividly.
For all to see and hear,
they shook my hands,
kissed 'Mnca-mnca' and hugged me;

calling me 'Comrade Poet extraordinaire!'
hanging political blah on my oeuvre.

I mourned about proposals
getting lost in the labyrinth of funding,
'Obstructing non-praise poets
effects death of a language –
garroting of our humanity.'

As if I had the old, they gave me
new business cards. 'Now please,
Comrade Poet, email all,' they crowed,
'direct to one of us!'

Thrice I sent emails and SMSs.
No word from the corridors.
Thrice I turned to the receptionist.
Only "Please continue holding,
your call is important to us …"

You sense something, something wormy
about these people? And surely, it always
turns out to be true.

In their nightmares,
they discuss people
and whisper:
'We hate the Boers,
We hate the British,
We hate the Portuguese,
We hate the Jews!'
Hate, hate, hate.
Yet they have no vision
without white supervision.

Just look at these …
Remember this one
who got rid of the woman
and children he got in exile? And this
one for stomach stapling,
who earnestly offered to process
funding if 50% to him
I would give as hard cash?

Like pink tongue and saliva,
pink tongue and saliva,
together now they are.
They would have been still enemies,
had it not been the oil magnate – Sheik
Abdullah ibn al-Khattab's intervention,
because he buggers them both.

Ha, ha, ha once more,
look into my eyes:

You are the one within me,
a diver discovers in the tranquility
of the underwater cave.
I am the one within you,
a climber discovers on the crown
of Mount Kilimanjaro.
We are a birdsong, a snow crystal, a crop circle,
toothless giggles of a toddler on a beach.

HERE

Here we have smoked away all forms and voices of life.
Our dumb river, like a faint, very faint path, drags itself
timidly across the city. What roar are walls
as we jostle our way to relieve fellow breadwinners.
What chatter are computers and mobiles
playing with the unseen, reliving our childhood.
What hiss drives faeces and urine down
under our feet. What hoot are wheeled coffins
carved for Kyalami and the freeways.
No time for shy cockroaches. Ours are two-legged –
just to spite our Mayor. Then the keepers of law
and order, in snowstorms, burn rags, and
with teargas fumigate crevices.
       Here we all die from want, cold, loneliness, diseases,
overwork, overcrowding. Corpses and carcasses live long
in coolers, longing for the last ceremony to the bowels.

       Here the flowers grow in urns. Their gnarled roots grope
upwards gaining leaves and flowers of their own. Small men
joltingly masturbate from balconies. Guided semen,
for inventive insemination, splashes via heads and shoulders
of passers-by. In corridors of trade, a troupe of gangly boosters
with plain grins, promenade around
as if the floors they tread are queasy. Bingo!
After a short interval – strip dance and … extras
dubbed "sex engineering" by the newly rich
perishing from obesity in private villas.
       Here, their sadists slap the crinkled, newly-born, cut it
from the mother, tie it, without remorse, to itself.
Babies and their counterparts – the toothless wrinkles grow
apart in quarantine to avoid exchanging word of earth,
word of the hereafter. Without shame we lock juveniles
in jails or nuthouses as premature psychotics. Sies, nx!

SOMETHING THE DEAD KNOW

*Chain poem by Angifi Dladla, Mika Linn and Matodzi Ramashia
performed in 2008 at the Jozi Festival. Outcome of a workshop by
Angifi at the University of the Witwatersrand.*

From Dafur,
Somali, Congo, Malawi,
Maputo, Zimbabwe – all black
north of opportunities   we run
barefooted, barehanded, and
backwards; not as cowards –
We are rams
gathering strength,
stamina …

Something the dead know
is the heat of the southern sun
bending the backs of brothers
unarmed.

Oh, heavenly South!
today, with a matchbox
and a garden fork,
you toyi-toyi in the footsteps
of the comrades – you loot,
burn my shop, stone, fork me to the street
and ram a tyre around my neck:

'Vele awafe ama kwere-kwere!
Sure, let the foreigners die!
Ay' hambe im dlwembe yama grigamba!
Let the feral foreigners leave our country!
Thelani le nja nge phethroli, isi-UDF!
Douse this dog with petrol, UDF-style!'

'Eat me now;
your biltong –
for tomorrow
a Shangaan, a Venda
is next …'

Blazing
Whirling
Defiant

Something the dead know
is the writhing of a maggot
in a cold, cold body
burnt blacker than black:
'Now you are too black
for my country!'

Tonight, the simmering
smell of charred screams
lull the children to bed:
'Bam' shisile,
they've burned him alive.
Bam' othile,
they've necklaced him
and danced around.'

Something the dead know
is the head held in broken hands;
the drooping mouth-hole,
a white speck of eye
leaking a tough sort of shame,
a burnt rubber which blackens blackness
and wires which swaddle the victim
like a Pharaoh.

Something the dead know:
Bones whiter than white
shall inherit the earth.

POET'S REPORT TO FIFA

And so the sons and daughters of Mother Earth
descended on our airports.
How pleasing to the soul witnessing
global smiles brightening up our cities.

And so used to navel-gazing
we could not believe our eyes.
How pleasing to the soul witnessing a ball
rounding off colours and tongues to One Family.

And so the FIFA Contest started.
Clans and tribes from all pockets of the globe
roared and buzzed with vuvuzela in our hives.
How pleasing to the soul witnessing stars dazzling our sky.

It felt like an African wedding: Bride
challenges bridegroom for a dance; crowds
ululate and whistle.
Zuri sana, we all dance and win!

And so the FIFA Contest went on.
Aficionados groaned, swore and threatened.
Losers broke and drooped,
sobs shrunk them away for a hara-kiri.

And so desolate
sons of Mother Earth packed their bags.
How paining to the soul witnessing a toy
whittling down, weeding out boys from the World.

And so the FIFA Contest rolled.
Victors hugged one another into a ball,
waved, swung, waggled and swaggered around.
Grossartig! Feu de joie! Grossartig!

And so FIFA Con test left us
with stillborn Zakumi and Diski-dance.
What a rich harvest of red ants and
new shantytowns we won.

A PEOPLE'S CONSTITUENCY

Today all denizens are outside,
shifting with scanty shades.
Half naked kids play in makeshift streets
that lead into syringes, as if to the shades.
With those ribs dusted and dabbed,
a drunk sailor can deliver a lovely shanty.

No latrine, no tap, no shower.
Kids shit like rats, women like cats.
The place smells of refuse, fermented beer
and carcasses of dogs and cats.

No school, no library, no newsvendor. Adults read birds
of paper scraps; kids dream of texts never will they get.

No bee, no butterfly; but flies from offal vendors.
A square metre in front for mealies and pumpkins.
A goat and two chickens here and there seem to be totems.
A reminder of the Bantustans.

No sign, no billboard, no shack number, no transport.
What's doing a compass job is a polling station;
brain-child of the People's President.
If no elections, denizens pose there for photos.

You dare claim these are images of his regality,
the fatted youth far in the township
can kill, serially for him; for he suffered,
seriously for the African masses.

MARIKANA CHORUS

ACT ONE
Opera Fiela lo Pikinini

Enter the Commissioner of Police with her ensemble.

O you misled strikers, wearing blinkers;
stop assembling on that privately-owned hill
brewing up division, friction, ill will.

Come back to your tried and tested federation,
your recourse is a tried and true reconciliation.

Good boys from our Reserves and beyond,
listen to what is beyond your rural minds,
listen to what will make your headmen mad:

A brainchild of a woman,
this pseudo-union,
funded by Western women
capitalists, this shady AMCU:

To divide and weaken COSATU,
to remove from the face of the earth NUM,
to disrupt our Neo-Liberal Project –
for a regime change, back to capitalist rule.

Come back to the revolutionary federation,
that led to our country's true liberation.

Dammit, you are not sensible,
you are not grateful. Who do you
think you are, tribesmen, depriving
your headmen of their revenues?

Constipated illiterates, glutted with loaves
of cockle bread, you fart around our hill, around
as if cockroaches have encroached onto your ears.
What do you think you're doing, under
the petticoat government, calling us
'Good marchers but bad leaders'?

Mark my word, you'll face the might,
the might of the People's Police Force.

No village picaninny can intimidate us,
we have defeated De Klerk and his apartheid.
No tenant picaninny can intimidate us,
we have defeated Terreblanche and his right wing.

No one can drive a wedge between us and Lonmin.
No anarchist can retard this homegrown reconciliation.
We'll crush and pulverize for Developer Lonmin.
This country needs native capital for modernization.

Your AMCU is a small cockroach,
it needs a mild spray or a toddler's toe.
It is toothless, noisome like an anus.

Today is D-day – the end
of this criminal act.
Today is your hour – the finale
of this dastardly venture.

Come on SACP and COSATU,
close ranks, isolate, petrify AMCU.
Come on People's Storm Troopers,
encircle these bastards in the manner
that you are trained to do.

I give you a helicopter, razor wire,
rottweilers, horses, machine guns.
Come down hard on these dissidents.

Shoot the magodukas, shoot merafes,
execute these fucken migrants!
Let our thunderbolts shame
the magic of their witchdoctors!

Come on, each shot be a kill-shot.
One, Two, Three: FIRE …!

Bham-bham! Qhu-qhu! Boom-boom!
Ra-ta-ta-ta-ta …!
We aimed, they fell, they glutted
the morgues.
Aha-ha-ha-ha …!

Bham-bham! Qhu-qhu! Boom-boom!
Ra-ta-ta-ta-ta …!
We aimed, they fell, they glutted
the morgues.
Aha-ha-ha-ha …!

ACT TWO
Ritual

*Wailing of women, some hysterical … Enter the elders – men
and women – each wearing a set of senonnori chains: Left hand
between the thighs, right hand at the back, towards the thighs
– joined by handcuffs. They perform, in their tongues and in
Fanakalo, variations of the ritual – to the spirits of the massacred.
Wailing continues in the background …*

ACT THREE
Remembrance

*On the Hill of Tripartite Mandate – looms large a statue of
Mgcineni Mambush in a green blanket. Below him a relief of
a man kneeling, praying; and of the massacre. Candles and
flowers ... Enter the ragged miners, solemnly singing 'Uthi, sixole
kanjani?' They kneel, burn impepho incense, sprinkle the snuff,
clap hands rhythmically as they talk to the spirit people ... Around
the monument they empty their hearts in dance.*

Marikana, Marikana,
the name Marikana
reprises storm troopers,
boring through skins
of our forefathers.

Marikana, Marikana,
the name Marikana
tastes like tears of old
streaming from new
widows, new orphans.

O Marikana, Marikana,
you are a re-vision
of TRAGEDY 1946,
by Ntate Sfaso's fountain
of gold – loaded from bodies
of black miners.

Marikana, Marikana,
tina ai funa lo New Apartheid.
World Trade Centre Accord
through TEBA and the barracoons
never was for us workers.

Marikana, Marikana,
the name Marikana
sounds as Tank Zonkana
Senzeni-Na, loud-speaking
for our death-day.

Marikana, Marikana,
lo mehlo bona muhle manje:
Qim qekelele Lo-Mina kolonali,
yena nqguza ga lo mbuzi.
Voetsek Baasboy Monare,
ga lo *Hamba kahle Pikinini.*

Marikana, Marikana,
we see more clearly now:
Blatant like a goat's fuck-hole,
is colonist Lonmin. Go to hell
Baasboy Monare, with your blood
money for burials.

Marikana, Marikana
you have cartwheeled us
from Cecil Rhodes' road
into a ghostly canyon.

Marikana, Marikana,
today you know what is not new:
'The driving force of civilization'.
Workers of England or Europe,
today you know what is not new:
Our blood relations, O Engels!

HAPPY BIRTHDAY

Happy Birthday our President,
Happy Birthday Mongameli,
Happy Birthday Honourable One.

We bring you barrelfuls of tears,
We bring you widowed tears at least,
We bring you barrelfuls of blood,
We bring you gunned down blood at least.
We bring you barrelfuls of pus
as thick as urine,
as thick as reptile urine.
All cargoes are from provinces,
all nine are orphaned;
all with no Medicaid.

How old are you now?
How old are you now?
How old are you now
if we look older than yourself?

We bring you coachfuls of bones,
We bring you senior citizens.
All are spotless,
all are dry-cleaned.
Thanks to scruples,
thanks to industry
of your white-collar vultures.
We bring you bones,
We bring you winged bones
that do not have any marrow.
Our young are sticks,
our young are makeshift sticks
if senior skeletons don't want to fly.

All freights are from provinces,
all boxcars carry bone charcoal,
all provinces rattle a happy birthday.

Ukhule Mongameli, ukhule unga khokhobi.
Grow older our President, grow older without stooping.
Ukhule Mongameli, ukhule unga khehlezi.
Grow older our President, grow older without rattling.

Here is our ensemble,
the Azanian Ensemble
rattling the *Mother of all Birthdays*.

Give our regards up North,
give our regards to our Developers
as you indulge in caviar and undersea-stored wine.
Give our regards up in Davos,
give regards to your presidential brothers
as you sign amazing deals.

BAYEDE

Bayede, Son of man, Bayede!
You who outsmart the invisible God of our ancestors,
You who perfect the creations of the One-Who-Cannot-Be-
    Imagined.
Modernizer of flying dragons that drop eggs down on cities –
They whose eggs hatch bouncing chicks, enveloped in
    clouds with no linings.
O Inventor of plague-like rain and diseases,
What a mutagen of nature you are!

Bayede, Son of man, Bayede!
With lashes and nails, Jesu surrendered to your cross,
With a red stroke, sons of heaven rot to die in your jails,
With omission and neglect, sages die muzzled and
    forgotten.
Yes! You appraise absolute truth and belittle the God of our
    ancestors.
Yes! You sentence God to eternity in your prisons.
What a demystifier of God you are!

Bayede, dredge of ocean and land marrow, Bayede!
You who imprison nature and charge for entrance,
You who farm waste to fertilize the sky and the soil and the
    waters,
You who crack cells and sells us mutants for cyborgs.
Colonizer of oceans, You'll soon reside under the ocean,
Colonizer of space, You'll soon drill the Moon and Mars,
Build supermaxes and nuthouses up there.
Yes! as God-shrike, You'll lynch angels and the sons of
    heaven up there, yes!

But look, O youngest brother of Mu, just look:
We are on the brink of taking a Cosmic Route.
Look, O man who inherited breast milk from Atlantis,
O, no-no, don't borrow Madam Lot's eyes.
Look, and listen to your heart: The voice within
is the call of the Cosmic Brotherhood!

VISITATION

On the western and southern sides of the arena are mabele, teff,
poone, serowe, amadumbe, izindlubu, and other vegetables in the
field of Goddess Nomkhubulwane. On the eastern and northern
sides is a forest. Within iguma (reed entryway), women roast
various nuts and display homegrown and wild fruits. Others at
a distance cook vegetables, fish, beef, mutton and meat of goat.
Game, chicken, partridge, ostrich, etc. are on spits. Adding to the
aroma and impepho incense are different kinds of tea and coffee;
soft drinks, beer and wine.

There are four gates, whose entranceways are polished with cow
dung. Before each gate there is isivivane – mound of small stones
brought by everyone from their respective lands. Megaliths housing
our past and that of the gods surround the arena. Some have
engravings and paintings depicting the gods, stars, planets together
with mysterious forms of writing; others are mounted with giant
masks, a few are sculptures. Spectators sit on terraces. Kids in front
next to the centre.

In the navel of the arena is a slightly raised platform of knitted
stones in the form of isicoco, headring. Fireplace, The Throne
of Light. Light bathes the whole area. Around The Throne of
Light drums are being warmed. On the eastern side next to the
spectators, eight musicians sit behind the marimbas. At the back a
man with a kora is ensconced on a high granite stool. On his side
two masked men with talking drums, an umondo and gangan;
next to each one with a sekere and the other with a kayamb.

Strums of the kora, bobre, nyanyeer and gorah …

Enter the griots from gate one, simultaneously with a djembe
drummer in gate two, another in gate three, followed by Rwandan
dancers. From gate four emerge sega dancers from Mauritius.
Marimbas join in.

Enter dancers playing didgeridoos and others from very icy
regions, followed by Brazilians from gate four playing their own.
Then the Dancers of God from the rainforest, simultaneously with

those from Asia and all over the Black Worlds.

*Today is the fifth day of the Ncwala-Chinamwali Festival,
or Harvest Celebrations, extended into the Rebirth of the Black
Worlds.*

*As moonlight filters through the trees, two women perch on the
branch of an imposing tree strum a ndomu and umakhweyana.
Moonlight gives them and their sound a celestial aspect. They are
joined by all musicians. All spectators rise up. They sing the ancient
Anthem of the Race ...*

*After the opening by a Vudun High Priestess from Haiti and
the men wearing masks beat the talking drums crying for the
Rebirth of Alkebu-Lan and the arrival of Nu and Nut, Amma
and Nummo, Demania and Demazania – Twins of Heaven. They
gradually slow down as they hear ululating and clapping ...*

*Enter tiny people – men and women, men wearing caps of
horns and each holding a nqu-tail switch and bonewhistle in their
mouths. Heartening, uplifting, celebratory dances. Two dancers in
a trance, a deep trance. Their ncum energy boiling, rising!*

*Rumbling footsteps and sounds of otherworldly musical
instruments distantly. Musicians, dancers and spectators crane
their necks.*

Exit tiny people carrying the trancers.

*Enter the visitors, men and women, resplendent in their robes.
Music in the background seems to come from the stars and the
horizon.*

We come from the ancient kingdoms
We come from Kush and Ta-merà
We come from Aksum and Punt
We come from Mali and Ghana
We come from BuKongo and Azania.

We come with divine resonance
from the Great Falls of Mosi-oa-Thunya
We come with the flute of light
from Fundi Akuffu-Ankh.

We come with the hallowed harp
from the Great Temple of Kush
We come with a primordial drum
from the Bowels of Mount Meru.

We have come to your festival
We have come to celebrate poetry
We have come to celebrate storytelling
We have come to celebrate performance.

We come with perfumed songs like the laughter of flowers
of Mount Kilimanjaro and Mount Goerikwaggo
We come with cycloid strokes like purls
from the hallowed well of Ngome.

We are not a race of today,
our epics are told in light years.
We are not a race of yesterday,
we have witnessed worlds created, destroyed.

We have seen Proserpine cut with a beam
We have seen Mars turned into dust
We have seen Lemuria exploded and sank
We have seen Atlantis ripped apart and drowned.

We have fought and won galactic wars
when madness almost shook the pillars of the universe.
We have fought and won galactic wars
when Planet Earth was still not yet born.

We have witnessed Gardeners of Forms plant Life
We were here when the sun rose from the west
We were here before the arrival of the moon
We were here before the age of ice.

We are here to celebrate the Word
We are here to celebrate Service
We are here to celebrate a Vision
We are for the Cosmic Brotherhood itself.

We come with cosmic light from the copper city
under the Mountains of Ruwenzori
We come with sublime harmony
from the confluence of Khoe-San oceans.

We come with a final dawn:
The call-chorus of the universe
from the hidden tomb
and the Great Sphinx.

We usher in Head-spirits from Tsodilo Hills
down the Kgalagadi, friends from underground cities
and caves. They come with you visiting from the future,
and with guests from galaxies beyond.

They all come with divine silence
like silent songs of Lake Fundudzi
and the underworld waters of Lesotho.

Only the Enlightened Ones among you can hear
and understand the language of light and silence.

Witness the spectacular, O Enlightened Ones, as they walk
Poets, Performers and Tellers of Tales to the field!
Listen to the Guests of Honour impressing on them:
'Courage, Poets and Tale-Tellers, Courage!
Courage, Performers and Masters of Rhythm, Courage!
The centre is yours.'

Listen to King Akuffu and the legendary Aesop
Listen to the voices of old, always new
Listen to Juan Latino, listen to Magolwane, listen to Tsegaye
Listen to Mnyampala, listen to Mqhayi, listen, listen to Maya
    Angelou
Listen to Aimé Césaire, listen to p'Bitek, listen to Kouyaté
Listen to Viera, listen, aah, listen to Dennis Brutus!

Listen to Akhenaten and the legendary Kheti
Listen to profundity of old, always sparkling
Listen to Hassan, listen to Antar, listen to McKay
Listen to Manzano, listen to Baraka, listen, listen to
    Langston Hughes
Listen to Muyaka, listen to Mapanje, listen to Ingoapele
Listen to Waaqoo, listen, aah, listen to Mazisi Kunene!

Now is the moment;
the great moment
we have been waiting for.
Let miracles begin,
let life prevail,
let stories roll,
let drama flare up,
let poetry explode,
                resound …!

NOTES ON THE POEMS

p12 **Baasboy**: Black foreman supervising his fellow black workers. In turn he is supervised by Baasie, a young white foreman, who reports to Makulubaas, the big boss

p13 **Kwasa-kwasa**: Dance music created in the 1980s by Jeannora in the Democratic Republic of the Congo. The dancers play in a masterful way with their hips and hands

p13 **Mbaqanga**: A cross between marabi and kwela music with a heavy influence of Zulu traditional music popularized by Mahlathini and the Mahotella Queens

p14 **Eita Blazah**: Hi, Brother

p18 **Moria**: "Mecca" of Amazayoni, home-grown Zionist Christian Church with traditional African beliefs

p20 **Phrrr**: Sound of a bird suddenly flying

p32 **Tasmanian devil**: A fierce marsupial carnivore the size of a small wild dog. It is not wasteful as it demolishes fur, skin, flesh and bones

p40 **Klevahs**: (Tsotsis) Township young thugs or gang members

p43 **Spook-mathambo**: Ghost with only its skeletal frame

p45 **Kgalagadi**: Kalahari Desert

p46 **Kiss-Madolo**: Knock-kneed person

p52 **Mango**: Mangosuthu Buthelezi, leader of Inkatha Freedom Party p52 **SADF**: South African Defence Force in the days of apartheid

p52 **PW Botha**: Apartheid president who announced his 'total onslaught' strategies in 1985 to his Cabinet, "We do not pretend like other whites that we like Blacks ... I have a committee working on finding better methods of inciting Blacks against each other and encouraging murders among themselves. Murder cases among Blacks should bear very little punishment in order to encourage them. My scientists have come up with a drug that could be smuggled into their brews to effect slow poisoning results and fertility destruction. Ours is not a war that we can use the atomic bomb to destroy the Blacks, so we must use our intelligence to effect this. Our Sex Mercenary Squad should go out and camouflage with Apartheid Fighters while doing their operations quietly administering slow killing poison and fertility destroyers ... We have received a new supply of prostitutes from Europe and America who are desperate and too keen to take up the appointments. My latest appeal is that the maternity hospital operations should be intensified. We are not paying those people to help bring Black babies to this world ... My Government has set aside a special fund for erecting more covert hospitals and clinics to promote this programme." *Sunday Times, 18 August 1985*

p54 **eMatrasini**: Chamber of mourning

p55 **Umdlezane**: Woman who has recently given birth

p63 **Izandla ziya gezana**: One hand washes the other

p67 **Dunusa Park**: Before the place became a squatter camp, it was a large open space where nearby hostel dwellers used to cleanse and detoxify their colons. Thus Thokoza residents called it Dunusa Park, "Protrude- Your-Buttocks Park". It had a maze of narrow streets with cul-de-sacs, as a deterrent to the police and soldiers. But later this shantytown was upgraded and became cozy, for the residents to *phola*, to settle comfortably undisturbed

p69 **Leper Island**: Africans called Robben Island by this name because lepers were exiled there

p69 **Jan se Gat**: Stone quarry in Robben Island

p69 **Makana, Autshumato**: Rickety boats named after two early Robben Island prisoners

p69 **Granma**: The name of the yacht Fidel Castro used in 1956 when he invaded Cuba to topple Batista Fulgencio. He also named a province and a Communist Party newspaper after this yacht

p69 **Autshumato, Makhanda, Sheik Madura, and other names**: Past political prisoners in Robben Island

P70 **Sobukwe Clause**: A special parliamentary decree to keep Robert Sobukwe, leader of the Pan Africanist Congress, in prison after his sentence had ended

p71 **Poqo Island**: The name Africans gave to the Robben Island in the 1960s because more than 1000 Poqo guerillas were imprisoned there

p73 **Mnca-mnca**: Sound made when kissing

p76 **Kyalami**: A motor racing circuit in Midrand, Gauteng

p77 **UDF-style**: In the 1980s youths affiliated to the United Democratic Front, UDF or Mavarara, used to terrorize black communities and make black areas ungovernable through an orgy of 'necklacing'. This meant ramming a tyre around the neck of an enemy (i.e., an African elderly, or a person affiliated to a different political organization), dousing him or her with petrol or diesel, and dancing around the flaming, screaming victim. These youngsters were euphemized as 'comrades'

p80 **Zuri sana**: Wonderful!

p81 **Grossartig**: Superb!

p81 **Feu de joie**: A celebratory rifle salute, each soldier firing in succession along the ranks to make a continuous sound

p81 **Zakumi / Diski-Dance** : Official mascot and football moves-dance of the 2010 Soccer World Cup

p81 **Red ants**: Notorious group of security guards in red overalls, inherited from the apartheid regime, who tear down illegally-erected shacks and remove squatters from illegally occupied building or land

p83 **Opera Fiela lo Pikinini**: Opera Sweep-Away the Picaninny

p83 **AMCU**: Association of Mineworkers and Construction Union

p84 **"Good marchers but bad leaders"**. Writing in 1905 about the Mensheviks, V I Lenin said: "Good marchers but bad leaders, they belittle the materialist conception of history by ignoring the active, leading and guiding part in history which can and must be played by parties that understand the material prerequisites of a revolution..."

p85 **Magoduka, merafe**: Migrant workers

p85 **Senonnori chains**: Apartheid version of a cangue or stock

p86 **TRAGEDY '46**: In August 1946, Jan Smuts' police killed Black mineworkers in the Witwatersrand

p86 **TEBA**: The Employment Bureau of Africa, the mineworker recruiting agency

p86 **Barracoons**: crude enclosures in which blacks were confined before they were transported to the Americas or elsewhere

p87 **Lonmin**: British owners of the platinum mines in Marikana

p87 "From the first day to this, sheer greed was the **driving force of civilization**." – Friedrich Engels, *The Origin of the Family*, 1894

p90 **Bayede**: Hail – salutary greeting or address to a personage with royal blood

p92 **Visitation**: This poem was first performed by the Akudlalwa Communal Theatre in 1990 at the Afrika Day Festival, Vosloorus Civic Centre

Printed in the United States
By Bookmasters